A Pocket Guide
to Written English

D1146952

A Pocket Guide to Written English

Michael Temple

John Murray

Also by Michael Temple

A Pocket Guide to Spelling

© Michael Temple 1978

First published 1978
by John Murray (Publishers) Ltd
50 Albemarle Street, London W1X 4BD

Reprinted (revised) 1979, 1980
1982, 1983, 1985, 1986, 1989, 1991

Printed in England by Clays Ltd, St Ives plc

0 7195 3508 5

Contents

Acknowledgements

I am grateful to my wife and colleagues for their valuable assistance and to my pupils, past and present, without whose errors I could not have written this booklet.

1 Spelling

(See also **Words often confused**, p.10)

General

Wide, attentive reading will obviously help with spelling, as with all matters of expression. Careful pronunciation and grouping words in 'families' may also help. It is a good idea to underline that part of a word which gives you trouble. Always check with a dictionary or the list of commonly mis-spelt words if you are at all uncertain.

It is best to learn a few spellings at a time and to know the 'rules' (see pages 5 to 9).

(a) Study the word carefully and pronounce it.
(b) Shut your eyes and try to picture the word.
(c) Check the spelling.
(d) Write it down from memory.
(e) Check it carefully.

ALPHABETICAL LIST OF THE MOST COMMONLY MIS-SPELT WORDS

(See Section 2 for words like affect/effect and council/counsel)

absence
academically
accelerate
accessible
accidentally
accommodation
achievement
acknowledge
acquaintance
acquiesce (in)
acquire
acquit(ted)

across
adaptation
address
adequate
advertisement
aerial
aggregate
aggressor
agreeable
alcohol
allege
allot(ted)

all right (2 words)
a lot (2 words)
already
altogether
amount
analysis
ancillary
annihilate
appal(ling)
apparatus
apparently
appearance

1

appropriate
Arctic
argument
article
assassinate
associate
as well (2 words)
attachment
attitude
author
awkward

bachelor
balloon
barrenness
basically
battalion
beautiful
beggar
beginning
believe
benefited
bicycle
boisterous
burglar
business

calendar
campaign
careful
carefully
caricature
carriage
catarrh
category
caterpillar
cemetery
century
chaos
character
chief
cigarette
circuit

collaborate
colleague
college
colonel
commemorate
commission
committee
comparatively
comparison
competent
completely
conceive
concentrate
condemn
conjure
conscience
conscientious
conscious
consensus
consistent
conspiracy
contemporary
coolly
correspondence
corroborate
counterfeit
courteous
criticism
cruelly
curiosity
cynicism

deceit
decision
defence
defensive
definite
degradation
democracy
descendant
descent
description
desiccated

despair
desperately
detached
deteriorate
deterrent
develop(ed)
development
diarrhoea
difference
die, dying, died
difference
dilapidated
dilemma
disappear
disappoint
disastrous
discipline
disillusioned
disobeyed
disservice
dissolve
duly

ecstasy
eerie
eighth
elegant
embarrass
emperor
endeavour
enormous
environment
equatorial
estuary
exaggerate
exceed
excellent
except
exceptionally
excitement
exercise
exhibition
exhilarating
existence

expense
experience
extraordinary
extravagant
extremely
exuberant

Fahrenheit
familiar
family
favourite
feasible
February
fiery
fluorescent
foreigner
forfeit
fortunately
forty
fourteen
friend
fulfil
furniture

gaiety
galloped
gauge
goddess
government
governor
grammar
grandeur
grievous
guarantee
guard

handkerchief
harass
heaven
height
heir
hero, heroes
hindrance
horizon
humorous

humour
hungrily
hygiene
hypocrisy

identical
illegibly
immediately
imminent
in between (2 words)
incidentally
independence
in fact (2 words)
infinite
in front (2 words)
innocence
innuendo
inoculate
in spite of (3 words)
install
instalment
insurrection
intellectual
intelligence
intention
interested
irregularly
irrelevant
irreparable
irresistible
irreverent
isosceles

jealous
jeopardy
jewellery (or jewelry)

keenness
knowledgeable

laboratory
laid (never layed)
leisure
liaison
lieutenant

lightning (flash)
likelihood
literature
loathsome
loneliness

maintain
maintenance
manageable
manoeuvring
marriage
marvellous
mathematician
meant
medicine
medieval
   (or mediaeval)
Mediterranean
messenger
metaphor(s)
mimic(ked)
miniature
minute
miscellaneous
mischievous
monastery
murmured
murmuring
mystifying

naive
navigable
necessary
negligent
negotiate
neighbour
ninth
no one (2 words)
noticeable
nuisance

occasionally
occur(red)
occurrence

offered
old-fashioned
omission
opportunity
ordinarily
originally
overrule

paid (never payed)
panic-stricken
paraffin
paralleled
paralysed
parliamentary
particularly
pavilion
peculiarly
permanent
permissible
pigeon
playwright
poisonous
possession
precede
predecessor
predilection
preferred
prejudice
preparation
presence
pretence
pretension
primitive
privilege
probably
procedure
proceed
professor
programme
pronunciation
proof
propeller
protrude

prove
psychiatrist
psychology
publicly
punctuation
pursue

quarrel(ling)
quarter
queue
quietly

really
receipt
receive
recommend
reconnoitre
refer(red)
referee
reference
referring
refrigerator (fridge)
religious
reminiscence
repetition
reservoir
resistance
responsibility
restaurant
rhyme
rhythm
ridiculous
rogue
rouge

sacrilegious
sandal
satellite
scenery
scissors
secretary
seize
sentence

separate
sergeant (or serjeant)
sheriff
silhouette
similarly
simile(s)
sincerely
skilful
soldier
solicitor
soliloquy (-quies)
souvenir(s)
sovereignty
speech
statistics
subtlety, subtly
successfully
summarize (or -ise)
supersede
surfeit
surprise
survivor
symmetry
systematic

technical
technique
temperature
temporary
tendency
terrifically
terrifying
tobacco
toboggan
tomorrow
tongue
tragedy
tragic
tranquillity
tries
truly
twelfth
tying

tyranny	vehicle	wield
	vengeance	wilful
undoubtedly	veterinary	wiry
unnecessary	vicious	withhold
until (but till)	vigorous	witticism
	villain	woollen
vacuum	virtually	worshipped
valley(s)		
valuable	weird	yacht
vegetable	wholly	yield

SOME HELPFUL RULES

1 'i' before 'e' except after 'c', if the sound is 'ee'

e.g. believe, achieve, chief, siege, deceit, receipt, ceiling
(Exceptions: seize, counterfeit, weir(d), protein, plebeian, species.)
When the sound is *not* 'ee', the spelling tends to be 'ei':
e.g. neighbour, height, foreign, heir, forfeit. (but note: friend.)

2 Verbs ending in '-eed' and '-ede'

Double 'ee' must go with 'suc-', 'ex-', and 'pro-'.
e.g. succeed, exceed, proceed
Otherwise: intercede, precede, recede, concede.

3 'c' or 's'?

The noun has 'c'; the verb 's'.
e.g. a practice (noun)   to practise (verb)
     a prophecy (noun)   to prophesy (verb)
     a licence (noun)   to license (verb)
(It is worth remembering 'advice' and 'advise', which are pronounced differently.)

4 Doubling the letter before '-ing', '-ed' (and other suffixes which start with a vowel, e.g. '-er', '-est', '-able')

The final consonant is doubled before '-ing', '-ed', etc.

(a) in words containing a single short vowel (e.g. tap, hop):

e.g. hopping (short) as opposed to hoping (long)

Distinguish: shinning (up a tree), shining (sun)
         starring, staring; scarred, scared
         dinning (it into you), dining (room)
         dinner, diner (A diner eats a dinner.)

(b) in longer words where the stress falls on a *short* vowel at the *end* of the word:

e.g. begin(ning), occur(red), (p)referred, committed, admitted, fulfilling, regrettable, forgettable.

but *not* when the stress is elsewhere:

e.g. offer(ing), happening, benefitted, galloped, preference

(Exceptions: worshipped, handicapped, kidnapped.'

(c) in words ending in 'l' preceded by a short vowel, whether stressed or not:

e.g. travel—travelling; cancel—cancelled

(Exception: paralleled.)

5 Nouns ending in '-our'

These nouns drop the 'u' when forming an adjective in 'orous':

e.g. humour—humorous; vigour—vigorous; glamour—glamorous

(This does not apply to adjectives formed with the suffix '-able':

e.g. honour—honourable.)

6 Plurals

The general rule is to add an 's', or, after s, x, ch, sh, z, to add 'es'.

(a) If the noun ends in a consonant followed by a 'y', drop the 'y' and add 'ies':

e.g. fairy—fairies; monastery—monasteries;
    lady—ladies; ally—allies; story—stories

If the noun ends in 'ey', simply add 's':

e.g. donkeys, valleys, monkeys, chimneys, alleys, storeys

(b) Nouns ending in 'o', *except* for those listed below, add 's':

e.g. pianos, dynamos, photos

(The main exceptions: tomatoes, potatoes, heroes, mosquitoes, echoes, mottoes, torpedoes, cargoes, volcanoes, vetoes, embargoes, tornadoes, dominoes, buffaloes, desperadoes, haloes, noes.)

(Some have either: memento(e)s, innuendo(e)s.)

(c) Nouns ending in 'f' and 'fe'. There is no rule, though attention to the pronunciation helps:

e.g. calves, wives, knives, halves, shelves, thieves, loaves
    roofs, proofs, chiefs

Some have either:

e.g. hoofs/hooves, wharfs/wharves

(d) Some nouns keep their foreign plurals:

e.g. crisis—crises; oasis—oases
    criterion—criteria; phenomenon—phenomena
    terminus—termini (or -uses); larva—larvae
    medium—media (but mediums to contact ghosts)

(e) Hyphenated compounds usually add the 's' to the main noun part:

e.g. passers-by, sons-in-law, courts-martial

(Those formed from verbs take an 's' at the end:

e.g. lay-bys, lay-offs, take-offs, play-offs.)

(f) A few nouns have the same form in singular and plural:

e.g. sheep, aircraft

7 Words with prefix 'dis-' or 'mis-'

Do not add extra letters when a word contains the prefix 'dis-' or 'mis-':

e.g. dis + appear = disappear
    dis + appoint = disappoint

A double 's' will appear only when the word to which the prefix is added starts with an 's':

e.g. service   disservice
    spell   mis-spell
    satisfied   dissatisfied

8 Suffixes '-ful', '-fully'; '-al', '-ally'

(a) Adjectives formed with the suffix '-ful' or '-al' (e.g. careful, actual) have one 'l'

7

(b) When forming adverbs add '-ly' as usual:

e.g. careful   carefully
     beautiful   beautifully
     real   really
     accidental   accidentally
     actual   actually

(c) Adjectives ending in '-ic' form adverbs in '-ically' (except 'publicly'):

e.g. basically, terrifically, fantastically

9 Double 'll' becomes single 'l' in compound words

e.g. full + fill = fulfil
     skill + full = skilful
     already, altogether, always, although
     welcome, welfare

(See **Words often confused**, p.10: already and all ready; always and all ways; altogether and all together.)

10 Words ending in a silent 'e'

(a) These usually keep the 'e' before suffixes which begin with a consonant:

e.g. hopeful, arrangement, sincerely, completely

(Exceptions: argument, truly, duly, wholly.)

(b) If the suffix begins with a vowel the 'e' is usually dropped:

e.g. come—coming; argue—arguing; inquire—inquiry;
     subtle—subtly

but sometimes to keep the previous vowel 'long' the 'e' remains:

e.g. rateable, saleable

(Verbs ending in '-oe' do not drop the 'e':

e.g. canoeing, hoeing.)

(c) After words ending in '-ce' or '-ge' the 'e' must be kept so that the 'c'/'g' remains a 'soft' sound (i.e. as in Cecil or George, not 'hard' as in catgut):

e.g. noticeable, serviceable, manageable, courageous,
     singeing (burning)

(Contrast the pronunciation of singing, navigable, practicable.)

8

11 Words ending in '-y'

(a) Words ending in '-y' preceded by a consonant change the 'y' to 'i' before any suffix except '-ing':

e.g. cry   cried   crying
   try   tries   trying
   dry   dries, drier   drying
   satisfy   satisfied   satisfying
   hungry   hungrier, hungrily
   necessary   necessarily

(Exceptions: shyly, slyer, spryest, dryness.)

(b) Verbs like 'lie', 'die', 'tie' become 'lying', 'dying', 'tying'. (To 'dye' (clothes) becomes 'dyeing'.)

12 Words ending in '-ic' or '-ac'

These add a 'k' before '-ing', '-ed', '-er':

e.g. picnic   picnicking   traffic   trafficker
   panic   panicking   tarmac   tarmacked
   mimic   mimicked   bivouac   bivouacked

13 Prefixes 'fore-' 'for-'; 'ante-', 'anti-'

(a) The prefix 'fore-' means in front or beforehand:

e.g. forewarn, forecast, forestall, foreground

(Contrast: forbid, forbearance.)

(b) 'Ante-' means before; 'anti-' means against:

e.g. ante-natal, ante-room; antidote, antiseptic

14 'Joins' within words

Do not add or subtract letters at the 'joins' within words:

e.g. keenness, unnecessary, overrule, interrupt, drunkenness, withhold

2 Words often confused

(See also **Common faults**, sub-section 10, p. 33)

accept	to receive
except	to omit, exclude; not including
accessary	one who aids (e.g. in a crime)
accessory	an attachment or extra (e.g. to a dress or car)
adapt	to adjust
adopt	to accept and approve, take as one's own
affect (verb)	to influence or produce an effect on
effect (noun or verb)	a result; to bring about or accomplish
aggravate	to make worse
irritate	to annoy, exasperate
alibi	fact or claim that one was elsewhere
excuse	apology offered
allowed	permitted
aloud	audibly, loudly
allusion (to)	casual or indirect reference
illusion	false impression or image; magician's trick
delusion	deception, mistaken belief
already	by this time
all ready	all persons (things) are ready
alternate	by turns
alternative	either of two possible courses
altogether	completely
all together	all in one place
always	ever, constantly
all ways	all directions or methods

amiable	likeable
amicable	friendly
amount	How much? (weight or money)
number	How many? (individual items)
astrology	foretelling the future by the stars
astronomy	science of the planets and stars
bail	security for a court appearance; on cricket stumps
bale	bundle; to jump out of a plane (as verbs, both mean to scoop out water)
bare	naked; to uncover
bear	to carry; an animal
beside	at the side of
besides	in addition to
board	plank, table; to receive meals; to go on board
bored	weary with tediousness; made a hole
boarder	lodger (with meals)
border	edge, limit
born	come into the world by birth
borne	carried, endured
brake	to put the brakes on (e.g. a car)
break	to shatter; interval
breath (noun)	air drawn into lungs
breathe (verb)	to draw air into lungs
Britain	the country
Briton	the inhabitant
broach (verb)	to open (e.g. a barrel or a subject for discussion)
brooch (noun)	an ornament
cannon	a gun
canon	a churchman; church law
canvas	coarse cloth for tent, etc.
canvass	to solicit votes, orders, etc.
ceremonial (adj. or noun)	of a ritual or ceremony, formal
ceremonious	too much concerned with formalities, showy

check	stop; test for correctness; pattern of squares
cheque	bank draft or bill
choose	(present tense)
chose	(past tense of to choose)
civic	of a city
civil	polite; not military (e.g. 'Civil Service')
climactic	of a climax
climatic	of climate
coarse	rough, harsh, crude
course	for racing, golf; the division of a meal; a series; 'of course'
compare	to point out similarities
contrast	to point out differences
complement	that which makes up or completes
compliment	praise
contemporary	existing at the same time as
modern	up-to-date
contemptible	vile, mean
contemptuous	showing or feeling scorn
continual	frequent, repeated (e.g. dripping tap)
continuous	connected, unbroken (e.g. stream of water)
council	an assembly
counsel	advice; legal adviser; to advise
credible	believable
creditable	deserving praise
credulous	inclined to believe; gullible
currant	small berry
current	now running, in general use; flow of water, electricity, air
decease	death
disease	illness
defective	faulty
deficient	lacking
definite	fixed, certain, clear
definitive	final, complete, thorough

dependant (noun)	one who depends on another
dependent (adj.)	depending on
deprecate	to express disapproval of
depreciate	to go down in value, rate less highly
derisive	showing contempt
derisory	deserving contempt
desert	barren place; that which is deserved; to abandon
dessert	sweet course in a meal
detract (from)	to lessen, take away from
distract	to divert (attention)
disburse	to pay out money
disperse	to scatter, spread (or vanish)
discover	to find something which was always there
invent	to create or devise something new
disinterested	neutral, unbiased
uninterested	lacking interest, not interested
draft	rough copy or plan; draw up a bill, money order; selection for army
draught	all other senses: e.g. air current; beer on . . .; ship's displacement; game of draughts
drawers	chest of . . .
draws	verb to draw; drawn games; attractions
dual	double, composed of two
duel	fight between two people
economic	of a country's finances; profitable
economical	being careful, thrifty
effective	having an effect; coming into operation
effectual	answering its purpose
efficacious	sure to produce the desired effect
efficient	competent; working productively
elicit (verb)	to draw out
illicit	not legal
eligible	fit to be chosen
illegible	indecipherable
emigrant	one who leaves the country
immigrant	one who enters the country

13

eminent	prominent, distinguished
imminent	threatening, near at hand
ensure	to make sure
insure	to take out an insurance policy
envelop (verb)	to surround or cover
envelope (noun)	for a letter
especially	notably, particularly
specially	for a special occasion or purpose
exceptionable	objectionable
exceptional	unusual
fact	a truth, actual happening
factor	a contributory element, cause
faint	to swoon; dim, indistinct, weak
feint	sham attack, or blow; pretence (both mean 'pale' in phrase 'faint/feint lines')
fatal	resulting in death
fateful	deciding one's fate
flaunt	to show off
flout	to express contempt for (e.g. authority), defy
flowed	past participle of to flow (water)
flown	past participle of to fly (birds)
foregoing	preceding, gone before
forgoing	giving up, abstaining from
formally	in a formal manner
formerly	previously
fortuitous	happening by chance
fortunate	having or bringing good luck
genteel	affectedly elegant
gentle	not rough
hanged	executed ('hanged by the neck')
hung	other uses of the verb to hang
hear	to perceive sound, listen to
here	at this place

14

hoard	store
horde	crowd
human	of man as opposed to animal or god
humane	compassionate, kind
idle	lazy
idol	object of worship
imaginary	of a thing that exists only in the imagination
imaginative	having a high degree of imagination
imperial	of an empire or emperor
imperious	proud, domineering
imply	to hint (speaker implies)
infer	to draw a conclusion (hearer infers)
impracticable	that cannot be put into effect
unpractical	not having practical skill; not suited to actual conditions
industrial	of industry
industrious	hard-working
ingenious	skilful in inventing
ingenuous	artless, innocent
intellectual	of the mind, having superior powers of reasoning; a person who is concerned with things of the mind (as opposed to feelings)
intelligent	clever
intelligible	clear, understandable
into	entering, inside (e.g. He went into the house.)
in to	(separate senses) (e.g. She came in to tell us the news.)
it's	it is (or it has)
its	belonging to it
judicial	connected with a judge or law court
judicious	having sound judgement
larva	caterpillar, etc.
lava	from a volcano
lead	metal; (present tense of to lead)
led	(past tense of to lead)
leant	(past tense of to lean)
lent	(past tense of to lend)

15

less	smaller in amount
fewer	smaller in number
lightening	making less heavy or less dark
lightning	a flash of
loath/loth	reluctant, unwilling
loathe	to dislike greatly
loose	to unfasten; not tight
lose	to fail to win; fail to keep
luxuriant	growing profusely
luxurious	very comfortable; self-indulgent
marshal (noun or verb	officer; to arrange in due order
martial (adj.)	of war or the army (court-martialled)
masterful	imperious, domineering
masterly	expert, skilful
maybe	perhaps
may be	e.g. it may be . . .
meter	gas, electric, parking (measuring machine)
metre	measure of distance; verse rhythm
momentary	short-lived
momentous	important
moral	right, virtuous; lesson from a story
morale	mental state of confidence
negligent	careless
negligible	small or unimportant
new	opposite of old
knew	past tense of to know
notable	worth noting
noticeable	easy to see, prominent
observance	obeying, paying heed to (a rule or custom)
observation	noting, looking at
official	connected with an office; authorised
officious	meddlesome
oral	spoken (of the mouth)
aural	pertaining to the ear
verbal	in words (spoken or written)

16

partake of	to take or share (food or rest)
participate in	to take part in
peace	opposite of war; quiet
piece	a portion or part
persecute	to oppress, harass
prosecute	to take legal proceedings against
personal	individual, private
personnel	employees or staff
plain	flat country; clear; undecorated; unattractive
plane	level surface; to shave level; tool; tree; aeroplane
pray	to worship, beg
prey	hunted animal; plunder
precede	to go before in arrangement or rank
proceed	to go along, continue
precipitate	hasty, rash
precipitous	steep
prescribe	to order, lay down as a rule
proscribe	to condemn, prohibit
principal	chief, most important
principle (noun)	truth, law, idea; code of conduct
quiet	silent
quite	fairly, very, completely
rain	water from the clouds
reign	a king's
reins	a horse's
raise(d)	to lift, make grow, increase
raze/rase	to demolish, level to the ground
rise (rose)	to get up or go up
recourse	'to have recourse to' (to resort to)
resource	source of supply; device; ingenuity
re-cover	to cover again
recover	to regain health, regain possession of
re-form	to form again
reform	to correct, improve

17

re-sign	to sign again
resign	to give up (e.g. a job or office)
respectable	worthy of respect
respectful	showing respect
respective	relating to each in order
review	survey, inspection
revue	a stage production
right	opposite of left or wrong; just claim or due
rite	ceremony (religious)
write	with a pen, etc.
scarce	of ordinary things temporarily not plentiful
rare	of things infrequent at all times
seasonable	suitable to the occasion or season
seasonal	occurring at a particular season
sensible	showing good sense
sensitive	capable of feeling deeply; responsive to slight changes
sensual	indulging the senses
sensuous	relating to the senses
sew	i.e. with a needle
sow	i.e. with seeds
shear	to shave, cut
sheer	steep; absolute; transparent; to swerve
sight	thing seen; faculty of vision
site	location, position, plot
sociable	enjoying company
social	pertaining to society
solidarity	show of support for, holding the same interest as
solidity	state of being firm, stable, or solid
stalactite	comes down from 'ceiling' of a cave
stalagmite	grows up from the ground
stationary	not moving
stationery	writing materials
stimulant	alcohol, drug
stimulus	incentive

18

superficial	on the surface, shallow
superfluous	too many, more than is needed
taught	past tense of to teach
taut	tight, tense
temporal	earthly (as opposed to spiritual or eternal)
temporary	not permanent
their	belonging to them
there	in that place; there is
they're	they are
threw	past tense of to throw
through	from one end or side to the other; by means of
thorough	complete, in detail; very careful
to	always used except for:
too	also or in an excessive degree ('too hot')
two	number
translucent	allowing light through but not transparent
transparent	that can be seen through
urban	of a town
urbane	well-bred, suave, civilised
waist	part of body
waste (noun)	rubbish, barren land
waive	to set aside, forgo (a claim, right, rule)
wave	shake or move to and fro; curve(s) of water, hair, sound, heat, etc.
weather	sunshine, wind, rain, etc.
whether	if
were	past tense of to be
we're	we are
where	in what place?
who's	who is (or has)
whose	belonging to whom
your	belonging to you
you're	you are

3 Punctuation

(see also **Useful terms**, p.51)

---

1 The full stop

(a) marks the end of a sentence (except for questions and exclamations). A sentence is a complete unit of sense which can stand on its own. (It may consist of only one word as in greetings like "Hello.", commands like "Stop." (where the 'subject'—you—is understood), and replies like "No.".)

To test whether a group of words is a sentence, you should read it out to yourself; if it conveys a complete meaning, then you can probably put a full stop at the end. However, you must check the next 'sentence' in the same way.

(b) indicates an abbreviation. (It is only essential where the shortened form does *not* contain the last letter of the word.)

e.g. Co.   etc.   i.e.   a.m. — *but*   Mr   Dr

(Full stops are often omitted in abbreviations formed from initial capitals: e.g. BBC, TUC, MP (plural MPs).)

A series of three dots marks a breaking off. It is also useful when you are referring to a long extract and wish to give the first and last few words only. (The omitted section is covered by the three dots.)

2 Capital letters are used

(a) at the beginning of every sentence.

(b) at the beginning of a passage of direct speech (see 6 below).

(c) for proper nouns (i.e. names of *particular* persons, places, things), and for months of the year and days of the week:

e.g. Jane, Everest, Liverpool, July, Monday

(d) for adjectives derived from proper nouns (especially places and people):

e.g. English, French, Victorian, Elizabethan

(except for common compounds like brussels sprouts and venetian blinds, where the adjective has lost its original emphasis).

(e) for the first and all main words in *any kind of title*:
    books, plays, poems (e.g. 'Far from the Madding Crowd')
    films, T.V. programmes (e.g. 'Panorama')
    newspapers and magazines (e.g. 'The Times')
    names of ships, houses, inns
    a person's title (e.g. Archbishop of York)
    the titles of institutions and businesses (e.g. Women's Institute)
    abbreviations of such titles (e.g. M.P.)

(f) at the beginning of each line of verse (except in some modern poetry).

(g) for the pronoun 'I'.

(h) when a noun is personified or considered as a grand abstract idea:

e.g. 'The Child is Father of the Man.'

(i) for 'He', 'His', when referring to God.

3 The question mark

This is used for all direct questions:

e.g. What are you doing?
    You will come, won't you?

but *not* for reported questions:

e.g. I wonder what he is doing.
    Ask him who did it.

(Don't forget the question mark at the end of a long question.)

4 The exclamation mark

This expresses some kind of astonishment or a sharp outburst or comment:

e.g. Fire! Fire!

It can also add a tone of humour or sarcasm:

e.g. You're a fine one to talk!

(Don't over-use it and don't use more than one at a time.)

21

5 Commas

The following rules cover the main uses. (You will find that there are many other optional uses which lend emphasis or give a finer point of meaning.)

Commas are used

(a) to separate words, phrases or clauses in a list:
   (i) a series of nouns
   > e.g.   His room was littered with books, pens, papers and maps.

   (ii) a series of adjectives:
   > e.g.   He was a quiet, gentle, unassuming man.

   When one adjective describes the other or when the last adjective is closely linked with its noun, there should be no comma:
   > e.g.   the deep blue sky; a new Cambridge college
   > (Contrast: a thin, white hand)

   (iii) a series of adverbs:
   > e.g.   Try to work quickly, confidently and efficiently.

   (iv) a series of phrases:
   > e.g.   We spent an enjoyable day visiting the zoo, rowing on the lake, and picnicking in the park.

   (v) a series of verbs or clauses:
   > e.g.   He took a long run-up, slipped on the wet grass, and landed short of the sand-pit.

   (It is better with larger groupings to put a comma before the 'and'.)

The comma is also used between two long main clauses joined by 'and' or 'but', especially when the subjects of the clauses are different.

(b) before and after a phrase or clause in apposition (i.e. when placing a group of words after a noun to give a fuller explanation or description of it):

e.g.   Jean, *Bill's elder sister*, brought home a new hat, *a pink one with feathers*.

(c) to separate 'sentence adverbs'—these show the link between the whole sentence and the preceding one(s):

22

e.g. however, on the other hand, moreover
They tried hard. The conditions, *however*, were against them.

(d) to mark off the person(s) addressed or called to (whether by name or other description):

e.g. Look out, *Fred*! Now, *you fool*, you've missed it!

(e) to bracket off insertions or afterthoughts. (Dashes or brackets may also be used for this.) Use commas on either side of the parenthesis:

e.g. Sunday, *as everyone knows*, is a day of rest.

(f) to mark off interjections—words like 'yes', 'no', 'please':

e.g. *Well*, *er*, *no*, I don't think I will, *thank you*.

(g) before 'tagging on' clauses like 'don't you?' or 'isn't it?':

e.g. They played well, *didn't they*?

(h) to mark off a participial phrase:

e.g. *Seeing the lion*, Caesar screamed.

(i) to mark off adverbial clauses, especially when they start the sentence, except when they are very short. (Adverbial clauses are introduced by words like 'although', 'if', 'because'.)

e.g. *Although you may not realise it,* you need two commas in this sentence, *because it contains two adverbial clauses*.

(j) to mark off an adjective clause which merely comments but does not limit or define:

e.g. The boys, *who were fooling,* were punished.
(*Without* commas this would mean that *only* the boys who were fooling were punished; *with* commas it means that *all* the boys were fooling and were punished. The commas act like brackets.)

N.B. Don't put a comma between the subject and its verb:

WRONG: What he wrote, was illegible.
RIGHT: What he wrote was illegible.

6 Punctuating conversation/direct speech

(a) Start a new paragraph *every* time the speaker changes.

(b) The words spoken and the accompanying punctuation are enclosed in inverted commas (double or single). (N.B. The punctuation comes *inside* the inverted commas.)

23

(c) Even though the words spoken would form a sentence on their own, they are followed by a comma (not a full stop) when the verb of saying and its subject come *afterwards*:

e.g. "We are going away," they said.
but "Where are you going?" he asked.

(d) When the subject and verb of saying start the sentence, they are followed by a comma, and the first word spoken has a capital letter:

e.g. They said, "We are going away."

(e) When the 'spoken sentence' is interrupted to insert the verb of saying and its subject, one comma is needed when breaking off the speech and another immediately before continuing it. The next word within the inverted commas has a small letter, because it is continuing the spoken sentence:

e.g. "I am not," he stressed, "particularly happy about this."

Consider the following two sentences:

"I am going," he said. "Do not try to stop me."

7 Inverted commas are also used

(a) when quoting someone's words or from a book:

e.g. A famous speech from 'Hamlet' begins "To be or not to be".
(The full stop comes after the inverted commas. Contrast 6(b) above. No comma after 'begins'. Contrast 6(d) above.)

Take care, when quoting from a book/play/poem, that your own sentence leads naturally into the quotation.

(b) for titles of books, plays, T.V. programmes, films, newspapers, house-names, names of ships, inns, etc.:

e.g. Two of the most famous Elizabethan theatres were 'The Globe' and 'The Fortune'.

(Book or play titles may instead be underlined in writing, or italicised in print.)

(c) when using foreign words, jargon, specialist words or slang; or to show that a word is used sarcastically. (In print these might be italicised.)

N.B. Use *single* inverted commas within direct speech:

e.g. "Did you enjoy 'Pygmalion'?" he asked.

but if you use single inverted commas for speech—see sub-section 6(b)—then use double inverted commas within.

8 The apostrophe is used

(a) to denote *possession* with nouns. The singular noun takes an apostrophe followed by an 's'. Plurals ending in 's' add an apostrophe after the final 's':

e.g. a lady's hat, the ladies' hats (i.e. the hats of the ladies)
      a week's holiday, six weeks' holiday
      an ass's burden, Dickens's novels, Charles's sister
      Jones's cap, the Joneses' house (i.e. the house of the Joneses)

Be careful with unusual plurals (like men, children, mice) which are treated as if they were singular:

e.g. men's coats, women's rights, children's toys
      (*never* write mens' or childrens')

For proper nouns ending in a sounded 'e' and an 's' or in 's' vowel 's' (e.g. Euripides, Moses) add the apostrophe after the 's':

e.g. Ulysses' adventures, Archimedes' principle, Jesus' mother

(Note also—for goodness' sake.)

In units involving two or more nouns or in a compound noun or phrase, put the apostrophe on the last word only:

e.g. William and Mary's reign, my father-in-law's house, the Leader
      of the Opposition's speech

(This does not apply if there is no joint possession:

e.g. my brother's and my sister's birthdays.)

N.B. The apostrophe is *not* used in these words: yours, hers, ours, theirs or its (when it means belonging to it). (Would you write *hi's* for his?) It is, however, used in *one's* (belonging to one and one is/one has).

(b) to indicate a *contraction*. The apostrophe is placed where the letter(s) has(have) been omitted:

e.g. didn't, can't, they're (they are), you're, we're, I'd,
      I'll, it's (meaning it is or it has), fo'c's'le

(But note: shan't, won't.)

(c) for the plural form of certain *letters* and *figures,* although this apostrophe is now often omitted:

e.g. the three R's, P's and Q's, in the '60's, if's and but's

Do not put an apostrophe in ordinary noun plurals.

9 Dashes and brackets

Two dashes are used when breaking off a sentence to insert an afterthought or an explanatory comment or short list:

e.g. In August last year—I was with my family at the time—I had a serious accident.

Nothing—food, plates, cutlery, pans—could be left unattended.

A single dash may be used

(a) when breaking off a sentence for an abrupt change of thought or when 'tagging on' another construction:

e.g. The following day we had better luck—but that is another story.

(b) to emphasise a repeated word:

e.g. The new regime imposed rigid laws—laws which the police found difficult to operate.

(c) when bringing together a number of items:

e.g. Toothbrush, tin-opener, matches, scourer—these are often forgotten by inexperienced campers.

(d) with a colon to introduce a long quotation or list, although this usage is now dying out (this is called a pointer :—).

(e) to signify missing letters:

e.g. D – – – it!

Brackets (always two) are, like dashes, used for 'asides' and for enclosing additional information:

e.g. Citrus fruits (oranges, lemons, limes) are rich in vitamin C.

(Brackets, like dashes, often carry the meaning of 'that is' (i.e.) or 'namely'.)

(If there is a bracketed *phrase* at the end of a sentence, the full stop follows the bracket; if the brackets enclose a *sentence,* the full stop comes inside.)

10 The hyphen is used

(a) when attaching a prefix (e.g. multi-storey, anti-aircraft, by-product) and especially when confusion might result as with 're-sign' and 're-form'. (It also splits vowel sounds as in 're-elected'.)

(b) when forming a compound word from two or more other words:

e.g. son-in-law, a half-eaten biscuit, a couldn't-care-less attitude, red-hot, swimming-bath, smoking-jacket

Distinguish 'fifty-odd people' from 'fifty odd people'.

(The hyphen is also used when splitting a word between syllables at the end of a line.)

11 The semicolon is, or may be, used

(a) to separate clauses which could stand as sentences but which are *closely related*, especially

    (i) when the second clause *expands* or explains the first:

      e.g. Neither of us spoke; we merely waited in silence to see what would happen.

    (ii) when the clauses describe a *sequence* of actions or *different aspects* of the *same* topic:

      e.g. There was a sharp, bracing air; the ground was dry; the sea was crisp and clear.

    (iii) before 'sentences' beginning with 'even so', 'so', 'therefore', 'for instance', 'nevertheless', 'then', etc.:

      e.g. He took great care; even so, he made a few errors.

    (iv) to suggest a contrast:

      e.g. I like swimming; my sister hates it.

(In all the above examples full stops could have been used but would have been too abrupt.)

Note that the clause or 'sentence' after the semicolon always begins with a small letter.

(b) to mark off a series of phrases (or clauses) which themselves contain commas. (Compare the use of square and round brackets in mathematics.)

e.g. You will need the following: some scrap paper; a pen, preferably blue or black; some envelopes; and some good, white, unlined writing-paper.

12 The colon is used

(a) to introduce a list (e.g. as in 11(b) above), long quotation or speech:

e.g. Speaking at Caesar's funeral, Antony addresses the crowd: "Friends, Romans, countrymen . . ."

It may also be used

(b) before a clause which explains (often by illustration) the previous statement. The colon has the force of the word 'namely' or 'that is':

e.g. One thing is certain: we shall not surrender. (Here a dash could have been used.)

(c) to express a *strong* contrast:

e.g. God creates: man destroys.

(d) to introduce a climax or concluding clause:

e.g. After pondering the choices before him, he came to a decision: he joined the army.

(e) to make a pointed connection:

e.g. Jeremy became a director in just three months: his father was the chief shareholder.

4 Common faults

(see also **Useful terms**, p.51)

In a language which is constantly changing there is always some conflict between current usage and established practice. Similarly, there are differences between what is permissible in popular speech and what is expected in formal writing.

For a few of the constructions considered below there can be no hard-and-fast rules. (Such entries are marked with a †.)

1 Agreement

A singular subject must have a singular verb-form, a plural subject a plural verb-form. Be sure to ask yourself whether the subject is singular or plural.

e.g. *One* of the men *was* guilty.

A *range* of goods *was* available.

All along the coast *lie traces* of oil slick.

(a) Indefinite pronouns—i.e. 'anyone', 'someone', 'no one', 'none', '(n)either' (when used without '(n)or'), 'everyone', 'each'—are singular and should take a singular verb and be followed by 'he', 'him', 'his', and *not* 'they', 'them', 'their(s)':†

e.g. No one knows *his* own future.

Anyone can do it if *he* tries *his* best.

Each stood with *his* right hand behind *his* back.

(b) (N)either . . . (n)or. If *both* the subjects are singular, the verb is also:

e.g. Neither the man nor the dog *was* in sight.

If one or both of the subjects are plural, the verb is plural:

e.g. Neither John nor his friends *are* coming.

(c) this kind, this sort (or **these kinds, these sorts**), but not 'these kind', 'these sort'.†

(d) Collective nouns (which are groups of persons or things) take a singular verb when considered as a complete unit:

e.g. The class *is* too large.

but a plural verb when considered as a number of separate persons or things:

e.g. The class *were* quarrelling.

(e) The verb-form in an adjective clause must agree with the right noun (or pronoun) in the clause before it:

e.g. He is one of the most famous writers who *have* ever lived.
('Who' relates back to 'writers'; hence the plural 'have'.)

2 Case

(a) I, he, she, we, they, and **who** are the subject.

e.g. The man who will be king . . .

WRONG: John and me are brothers.
RIGHT: John and *I* are brothers.

WRONG: This is the man whom we all knew was guilty.
RIGHT: This is the man *who* (we all knew) was guilty.
(The brackets show that 'who' is the subject of 'was'.)
or: This is the man *whom* we all *knew to be* guilty.

(b) Me, him, her, us, them and **whom** are the object.

e.g. The man *whom* we met . . . (i.e. we met *him*.)

('Whom' seems to be dying out of the language, but should be kept after prepositions:

e.g. To whom shall I send it?
. . . for whom the bell tolls.

but not when *who* is the subject of a noun clause:

e.g. There was some doubt about who did it.)

WRONG: Thank you for inviting Joan and I to dinner.
RIGHT: Thank you for inviting Joan and *me* to dinner.

The object case is used after all prepositions:

WRONG: He gave it to John and I.
RIGHT: He gave it to John and *me*.

WRONG: between you and I; for you and he
RIGHT: between you and *me*; for you and *him*

3 The confusing of pronouns, especially 'one', 'you', 'it', 'he' and 'they'

(a) If you start using the word 'one' you must continue with it, though it can soon result in pomposity.

WRONG: One can easily spot your mistakes if you check carefully.

RIGHT: One can easily spot one's mistakes if one checks carefully.

(Or, better still, use 'you' and 'your'.)

(b) Make sure, when using pronouns like 'he', 'she', 'it' and 'they', that it is absolutely clear to whom or to what they refer.

WRONG: If the baby does not like fresh milk, boil it.

RIGHT: Boil the milk if the baby does not like it fresh.

WRONG: As the bomb fell into the car, it stopped dead.

RIGHT: The car stopped dead as the bomb fell into it.

(c) Do not confuse singular and plural.

WRONG: The marigold is a fairly hardy plant; they grow in most soils.

RIGHT: Marigolds are fairly hardy plants; they grow in most soils.

or: The marigold is a fairly hardy plant; it grows in most soils.

4 The comparative and the superlative

The **comparative** applies to two:

e.g. He is the better cricketer of the two.

The **superlative** applies to three or more:

e.g. He is the best swimmer in the county.

WRONG: John is the tallest of the two brothers.

RIGHT: John is the *taller* of the two brothers.

5 The participial phrase

This is introduced by a verb-form ending in '-ing' or '-ed' and describes the noun (or pronoun) nearest to it, but outside the phrase itself. Such phrases are often wrongly related, or unattached.

WRONG: Sitting on the veranda, the sun rose on our left. (This means that the sun was sitting on the veranda.)

RIGHT: Sitting on the veranda, *we* saw the sun rise on our left.

WRONG: Coming downstairs, the hall door opened. (This means that the hall door was coming downstairs.)

RIGHT: As he was coming downstairs, the hall door opened.

6 The gerund (or verbal noun)

This ends in '-ing' but acts as a *noun*; when qualified, it must, therefore, be preceded by an adjective (e.g. his, her, its, my, our, your, their):

WRONG: I don't like you leaving early.

RIGHT: I don't like *your* leaving early. (It is the 'leaving' I don't like.)

WRONG: I must escape without him knowing.

RIGHT: I must escape without *his* knowing.

7 The subjunctive

This is rarely used now, but watch out for:

(a) Pure supposition: e.g. If I *were* king . . .

(b) After verbs of wishing: e.g. I wish she *were* here.

(Also in 'Britannia *rule* the waves' and 'Long *live* the Queen'.)

8 The position of common adverbs (e.g. only, just, almost, even, mainly, also)

These should be placed immediately before the word they modify. Try inserting the word 'only' in every possible position in this sentence:

The bishop gave the baboon a bun.

(Consider the different meanings.)

Care must also be taken with the placing of 'both', '(n)either . . . (n)or' and 'not only . . . but also'.

WRONG: He not only plays tennis but also cricket.

RIGHT: He plays not only tennis but also cricket.

(The two parts must be correctly balanced.)

9 The correct preposition

(a) different *from* (or *to,* not 'than')

(b) to centre *on, in* or *upon* (not '(a)round')

(c) to prefer this *to* that (not 'than')

(d) anxious *about* (not 'of')

(e) bored *with* or *by* (not 'of')

(f) superior *to* (not 'than')

10 Words commonly confused

(a) Lie and **lay**. 'To lie' means to put yourself in a flat position; 'to lay' means to place something else (e.g. a plate) flat down.

To lie	*Present tenses*	I lie or am lying
	Past tenses	I *lay* or was lying
		I have *lain*
To lay	*Present tenses*	I lay it or am laying it down
	Past tenses	I *laid* it or was laying it down
		I have *laid* it down

(b) Shall and will

I/we *shall*, you/he/they *will* are the simple future tense.

I/we *will*, you/he/they *shall* express a strong wish or determination:

e.g. They *shall* not pass. I *will* not give in.

(A person intent on suicide might say: "I *will* drown and nobody *shall* save me.")

(c) May, might, can

'Can' means 'to be able to'.

'May' is the present tense; 'might' is the past tense. (Both mean 'to be permitted'.)

'May' also expresses a distinct possibility: 'might' expresses the idea that it is just possible but unlikely.

(d) Each other and one another; between and among

'Each other' and 'between' refer to two people or things; 'one another' and 'among' refer to more than two:†

e.g. In the duel they hurt *each other*.

The boys in the class were fighting *one another*.

(e) Due to and owing to

Use 'owing to' when you mean 'because of' and almost always at the beginning of a sentence. Use 'due to' (meaning 'caused by') as an adjective after the verb 'to be'.†

WRONG: Due to illness, he missed the game.

RIGHT: Owing to illness, he missed the game.

  or: His absence was *due to* illness.

(Many people feel that this distinction can no longer be drawn.)

33

(f) Like and as

'Like' is a preposition (or an adjective) but not a conjunction. It should not be followed by a finite verb. Use 'as' if you mean 'in the same way *that*':†

WRONG: He talks like I do.
RIGHT: He talks *as* I do.

(g) Past and passed

Use 'passed' for the verb (and its past participle); 'past' for all other uses:

e.g. He passed me the ball. He has passed.
in the past (noun); he went past (adverb); in past ages (adjective); he ran past me (preposition).

(h) Of, off, have

WRONG: I must of made a mistake.
RIGHT: I must *have* made a mistake.
('Of' is not a verb.)

'Of' means belonging to or relating to. 'Off' means away from or down from a place:

e.g. He fell off the cliff.

(i) Stood, standing; sat, sitting

WRONG: I was stood; I was sat
(unless you really mean that someone else picked you up and put you in a standing or sitting position)
RIGHT: I *was standing* or I *stood*; I *was sitting* or I *sat*.

(j) All right/alright

Some consider 'alright' to be all wrong: others think that it offers a useful distinction (meaning fairly well or yes) from 'all right' (meaning all are correct). Use 'all right' for examination purposes.†

(k) Should and would

The main uses are:

    (i) 'Should' or 'would' is used (depending on the person) as part of another verb expressing the future in the past:†
        e.g. I/we *should* be glad . . .
            you/he/she/they *would* be glad . . .

    (ii) 'Should', used with all persons, also means 'ought to':
        e.g. I/you/they *should* be playing in the team.

(iii) 'Should', also with all persons, is used for 'if' clauses:

e.g. If you should see him, give him my regards.

(iv) 'Would', with all persons, also expresses the idea of willingness:

e.g. I *would* play if I could.

(v) 'Would', with all persons, can also mean 'used to':

e.g. As a child he *would* play for hours.

11 Mixed constructions

(a) Faulty comparisons

WRONG: as good if not better than . . .
RIGHT: as good as if not better than . . .
  or: at least as good as . . .

(b) Double negatives:

WRONG: I don't want nothing
RIGHT: I don't want anything.
  or: I want nothing.

WRONG: He couldn't hardly believe it.
RIGHT: He could hardly believe it.

(c) Hardly/scarcely, when they mean 'no sooner . . . than', are followed by 'when' (or 'before'), not 'than':

e.g. He had hardly/scarcely written a page when/before the bell rang.

(d) Mixed tenses

WRONG: I should be glad if you will . . .
RIGHT: I should be glad if you would . . .
  or: I shall be glad if you will . . .

WRONG: I have and always will be a football fan.
RIGHT: I have been, and always will be, a football fan.

WRONG: I didn't ought to have done it.
RIGHT: I ought not to have done it.

WRONG: I didn't use to . . .
RIGHT: I used not to . . .

(e) Order of adjectives

WRONG: the three first chapters (there is only one *first* chapter)
RIGHT: the first three chapters (meaning chapters one, two and three)

35

(f) Try to/try and . . .
Normally use try *to*, except when you mean two separate actions:
e.g. Try to aim high or you may try and fail.

(g) Between is followed by 'and' (not 'or'):
e.g. He had a choice between cricket *and* tennis.

(h) Comprise (meaning 'consist of', 'be composed of') does not need 'of':
e.g. The kit comprised (or was composed of) four items.

(i) And who/and which occurs only if who/which has already been used in the sentence.

(j) Don't repeat a preposition
WRONG: These are the subjects to which he must pay attention to.

(k) Them/those
WRONG: Give me them slippers.
RIGHT: Give me those slippers.

12 Misused words

(a) Literally means exactly to the letter, in actual fact.
WRONG: He literally flew down the street. (He didn't sprout wings.)

(b) Unique means the only one of its kind—like the phoenix. Strictly, things can't be quite unique or very unique. (Likewise with 'invaluable' (meaning priceless).)

(c) etc. This is an abbreviation of *et cetera*, meaning 'and the rest'. It should not be used lazily; specify what you have in mind. Don't write 'and etc.', 'ect.' or 'e.t.c.'

13 Redundancy (using more words than are necessary)

WRONG: He is equally as clever as his brother.
RIGHT: He is as clever as his brother.
WRONG: He fell off of his horse.
RIGHT: He fell off his horse.

WRONG:	The reason why is because . . .
RIGHT:	The reason is that . . .
or:	This is because . . .
WRONG:	Long ago since . . .
RIGHT:	Long since . . .
WRONG:	You're nearer my age than what she is.
RIGHT:	You're nearer my age than she is.

'Assemble', 'co-operate', 'combine', 'mix' and 'mingle' do not normally require the word 'together'.

'Meet' is to be preferred to 'meet up with' and 'miss' to 'miss out on'.

Use 'just' or 'exactly', but not both.

'But' does not need 'however', 'yet' or 'nevertheless'.

'Return' does not need 'back'.

'As to' is often used unnecessarily, especially before 'whether'.

Avoid 'seeing as'—use 'as' or 'since'.

14 Mixed metaphors

These occur when you are not thinking and particularly when you are using overworked metaphors.

e.g. I smell a rat but I'll nip it in the bud.

15 Ambiguity (confusion of meaning)

This is often caused by:

(a) unclear pronouns:

e.g. She likes me more than you.
This could mean
either: She likes me more than she likes you.
or: She likes me more than you do.

Generally, ask yourself if it is clear to whom or what the pronoun refers, especially when you are using 'it' or 'they', and 'as' or 'than'.

(b) wrong punctuation or word order:

e.g. The door opened and a young woman carrying a baby and her husband entered.

(See also sub-sections 3 and 8 above.)

16 Words overworked or loosely used

(a) 'Nice', 'good', 'bad', 'lovely', 'fine', 'real', 'get'.

Over-using any word can cause monotony and blunt meaning, but the above are usually too vague or loosely colloquial for accurate writing, though they can sometimes be used with force. 'Get', though often too colloquial, may at times be the most natural expression. (e.g. He got off the bus.)

Other popular words which are loosely used are:

> fantastic, fabulous, tremendous, terrific, great, incredible, diabolical, ghastly, definitely

In general, look for a more precise word.

(b) In formal writing avoid colloquialisms and slang (i.e. expressions from common speech like 'lots of', 'bloke', 'a bit of alright', 'chickened out'). Avoid, too, loose, vague expressions like 'a good thing'.

(c) Clichés (i.e. very common over-used expressions) like 'this day and age', 'no way', 'the thin end of the wedge', 'stand up and be counted', and 'right across the board' should be avoided 'like the plague'!

(d) 'Then', 'so' and 'suddenly'. Often casually used or over-used by young writers, these words can cause disjointedness and dullness. Give more thought to varied, logical and effective sentence construction.

5 Notes on summarising (précis)

HINTS ON REDUCING THE LENGTH OF SHORT PASSAGES

The object is to put into your own words, simply and briefly, the essential ideas of the original.

1 Generalising

State the main points clearly, omitting details, examples and illustrations. (If the writer has used examples as his *only* means of expressing an important point, 'translate' them into a general statement.)

2 Re-casting sentences

Simplify sentences by making phrases do the work of clauses, and single words the work of phrases. (Omit sentences which merely repeat or illustrate a point.)

3 Figurative language

Avoid all figures of speech, expressing ideas in plain, literal language. Omit illustrative comparisons and contrasts.

4 Redundancy and repetition

Cut out unnecessary words and phrases; make a point once only.

METHOD OF SUMMARISING LONGER PASSAGES

1 Procedure

(a) Read through the whole passage to catch its general meaning. Then ask yourself what it is about. (It may help to give it a title.)

(b) Carefully re-read the passage, two or three times if necessary, to grasp its exact meaning. (At this stage briefly summarise the writer's basic line of thought.)

(c) Note down, in skeleton form, its essential points, paying special attention to the main parts of complex sentences, and to key sentences of paragraphs. (Omit purely illustrative passages.)

(d) Memorise these essential points (and the links between them), put the original passage and the notes aside, and do a first draft of the summary *in your own words*, in one paragraph.

(e) Revise this first draft, which may well be too long. Prune it of superfluous words and phrases, reconstructing parts of it if necessary. Refer to the passage if you need to, ensuring that you have not 'lifted' groups of words from it. Be sure that your version *connects* the ideas correctly (check link words such as 'but', 'therefore') and that it is not disjointed and telegraphic in style, but reads smoothly like an original composition. Combine sentences to save words, to establish the links between ideas and to achieve fluency.

(f) Write the fair copy, stating at the end the number of words it contains.

2 Notes

(a) Remember that the object is to give a true summary of the original. Add nothing of your own, and do not correct any factual mistakes the original may contain.

(b) It is usually advisable to follow the order of the original, but the ideas may be rearranged in any order, if this clarifies their logical sequence.

(c) It is not essential to use reported speech (third person and past tense) in every summary, but, if the original is written in the first person, the summary must make clear at the outset that someone else's views are being reported.

(d) The same techniques apply to a summary of particular topics contained *within* a passage. Pay careful heed to what is required before sifting the points.

6 Essays and compositions

SOME DO'S AND DON'T'S

Do:

(a) plan your material (on rough paper) and decide on the best approach and treatment.

(b) keep to the subject and make your meaning clear.

(c) develop the theme of each paragraph and link each paragraph to the following one.

(d) work out your sentences mentally before writing.

(e) choose words for their accuracy of meaning and aptness to context.

(f) vary the length and pattern of your sentences.

(g) give special care to opening and concluding paragraphs, making them as effective as possible.

(h) be prepared to work over and rewrite certain sections.

(i) finally, read through carefully, making necessary corrections clearly.

Don't:

(a) write what is too obvious or superficial.

(b) repeat yourself or 'ramble'.

(c) use slang or colloquialisms.

(d) write disconnected sentences or sketchy paragraphs.

(e) be unnecessarily pompous or affected.

(f) use several words where one would do.

SUGGESTIONS FOR DIFFERENT TYPES OF COMPOSITION

1 Formal essays dealing with ideas, information, arguments

(a) First jot down ideas freely for a few minutes, asking yourself plenty of questions.

(b) Look for an overall structure and approach: e.g. For and Against.

(c) Then sort out the best material under paragraph headings and in a logical sequence.

(d) Provide 'links' between your paragraphs.

(e) Remember that each paragraph is built on *one* main topic and should develop this fluently, usually with illustrative detail.

2 Descriptive and imaginative prose

(a) Train yourself to observe in a lively, accurate, honest way.

(b) Try to make the reader see, feel, hear and believe in the impressions you create.

(c) Use your imagination to perceive fresh likenesses (e.g. through metaphor and simile).

(d) Be economically suggestive—select only the most telling details.

(e) Choose words for the aptness of their associations and tone as well as for their precise meaning.

(f) Arrange your material to achieve *unity* of atmosphere, mood or viewpoint.

(g) Shape the rhythm and pattern of your sentences to your purpose.

3 Stories and character portraits

(a) Work out a clear storyline with a logical sequence of events. Don't pack in too many sensational incidents or follow conventional, hackneyed plots. It is often best to concentrate on a few centres of interest and on one climax, and explore fully the imaginative possibilities of these. Consider various different methods of telling your story—by first-person narrative, flashback, etc.

(b) Vivid, detailed descriptions of place, weather, etc. will help to create a convincing setting (and atmosphere) for your story. Sharp observation will help to make it real.

(c) Dialogue may help to create drama and atmosphere or illustrate character, but it can easily become flat unless you concentrate upon the feelings and reactions of the individual characters. Dialogue should, of course, suit character.

(d) Try to put yourself in the shoes of all your characters, considering their motives, feelings, reactions, and the interaction between characters. (It may help to start with a description of a person's physical appearance and then let character emerge through action and dialogue.)

(e) Once again, you need an overall design which integrates all the parts.

HINTS ON PREPARING FOR ENGLISH LANGUAGE ESSAYS IN EXAMINATIONS

(a) By the time of the examination you should know what *kind* of composition you normally write best (and worst!), e.g. narrative, descriptive, argumentative.

(b) After reading the questions carefully and thinking of interesting, original ways of treating them, make a *firm* choice; then forget about the others.

(c) Plan on rough paper, concentrating on finding a fresh, lively, personal approach, on developing and illustrating ideas, on building up a detailed and coherent imaginative picture. (Check for *relevance*. Avoid writing in slang or dialect.)

(d) Plan for about six paragraphs of roughly equal length for an essay of 450-500 words. Paragraphs which seem likely to be 'thin' or disjointed should be scrapped or worked over.

(e) Before writing, make sure your essay has unity of design—you may need to rearrange material or to provide links between paragraphs.

(f) Always leave time to correct your work.

GENERAL

Remember that most people write best about their personal experiences and that freshness and originality of approach are what make writing interesting and distinctive. Where possible, be yourself.

(The above notes are obviously no substitute for creative experiment, for the rich stimulus of good literature, and for constant practice.)

7 Notetaking and notemaking

These are essential skills for all students.

(a) The best notes are usually *short*.

(b) Note only *important* points or facts.

(c) Use *keywords* and *key phrases*.

(d) *Lay out* the notes usefully (a page with half-a-dozen spaced-out 'key phrases' may be better remembered and give a clearer sense of structure than a block of twenty lines of solid writing).

(e) *Read through* and, if possible, *pare down* the notes *immediately* after taking them.

(f) Picture or 'flow diagram' notes may be used in any subject because they

   (i) are *easier to memorise*.

   (ii) are *easily referred to*.

   (iii) can show immediately the *relationship* between topics, events, ideas.

   (iv) allow one to explore topics further, investigating new links between the key issues, arriving at new understandings.
(They may also be used *actively*—i.e. for problem-solving, creative thinking, essays.)

Using reference books

Scan with a pencil, ruler, bookmark. With practice this aids both concentration and memorising. A suggested procedure is:

(a) Check contents, index; look over the first and last chapters—the last chapter may be a summary of the book.

(b) Look over your selected sections, especially the first and last sentences of paragraphs, diagrams, tables, etc.

(c) Now look closely at the text, making your notes.

(d) (Very important) Go over your notes immediately after you have finished. Reject the unnecessary.

Memorising

To memorise notes, theorems, quotations, etc., try to write out the information *from memory* and then compare with the original notes. After notes and check-through have been made, revision should take place after an hour, then a week, then a month, or at similar intervals as convenient.

8 Formal letters

Letter-writing is a branch of good manners. You will often be judged on the letters you write—to prospective employers, for instance. The following notes apply to formal or official letters:

1 Paper

It is important to use *good*, preferably *white, unlined* paper (and to choose a size to match the length of your letter). It is always best to rough out your letter first—it can serve as your reference copy—as this will help you avoid mistakes, save expensive notepaper and give you an idea of the spacing and layout of the letter, enabling you to avoid crossings-out or signing off just over the page. Check your expression, punctuation and spelling. If you do make a mistake which requires crossing out, scrap the letter and rewrite the whole.

2 Addressing envelopes

Envelopes should match the paper.

(a) Layout

J. Blank, Esq.,	The Personnel Manager,
100 Blank Street,	John Murray (Publishers) Ltd,
BLANKTON,	50 Albemarle Street,
Blankshire,	LONDON,
PO2 8QT	W1X 4BD

Write a legible address with a postcode. (Punctuation at the ends of lines is not essential. You may 'stagger' each line of the address.)

Note: (i) Name/title of person and/or name of firm.
    (ii) Number (or name) of house and road name.
    (iii) Name of village or local district where applicable.
    (iv) Post town in CAPITALS.

    (v) County where applicable. Write it in full (or use the official abbreviation, e.g. Oxon.)

   (vi) Postcode in capitals, preferably on a separate line.

  (vii) Leave space at the top for the postmark.

(b) Warnings

    (i) Remember that you are writing to a particular person. Use his name or his office/title:

      e.g. The Registrar, The Principal, The Personnel Officer

   (ii) Write *either* J. Blank, Esq.
          or Mr J. Blank
       never Mr J. Blank, Esq.

    (Initials denoting qualifications, e.g. M.Sc., should follow the Esq.)

3 The letter

(a) Layout

Leave a margin space of at least 2½ centimetres down the left-hand side and at top and bottom, and 1½ centimetres down the right-hand side.

	(Your address	5 Blank Street,
	—like this or	Blankton,
	staggered)	Blankshire.

(Addressee)   (Date in full)   27 February 1977

The Registrar,
Leeds University,
Leeds.

Dear Sir,

....

....

Yours faithfully, }
             }→ (or centred for
(Signature)   }   written letters)

(The name and address of the addressee may instead be put in the bottom left corner, and, as on envelopes, punctuation at the ends of lines in addresses may be omitted. If you need to quote a reference number, put it in the top left corner.)

Notes on layout:

(i) Date in full, *not* 29.2.72 or Feb. 29th, etc., (but abbreviations for postcards).

(ii) 'Yours faithfully,' on the left-hand side below the message. (N.B. comma following.)

(iii) Beneath this, your signature *legibly* written.

(b) Mode of address and signing off

If you do not know the addressee, use 'Dear Sir,' and sign off 'Yours faithfully,'. If you know him, or have previously written to him, use 'Dear Mr Blank,' and sign off 'Yours sincerely,'. (No capital for 'sincerely' or 'faithfully'.)

(c) General

In general, aim at clarity, conciseness and dignity of expression. Be polite and direct. Avoid verbosity and business jargon (e.g.'We are in receipt of your highly esteemed favour of the 16th ult.'), as well as colloquialisms, slang and contractions.

If you are replying to a letter, you should normally first thank the sender thus: 'Thank you for your letter of 16 January.'

Start a new paragraph for your message. (It is common now, particularly in business letters, not to indent the first line of a paragraph. Instead, paragraphs are separated by spaces between them. This is also often done in books that consist of notes rather than continuous text—as this book does.)

When making requests, you will find the following a useful construction: 'I should be grateful if you would . . .'

When applying for a job, you could use a heading note before or after the 'Dear Sir,': e.g. Ref.: (Advertisement) in 'The Daily Globe', 12.10.77 (the date may be abbreviated in such cases).

(If you are writing to Lords, Queens or Bishops, you should consult a book of etiquette!)

In letters of a more friendly nature (not 'chatty' letters to the family) you may be more expansive and personal in style, but must judge the *tone* tactfully and adapt sensibly to the demands of the occasion. Think of the impression your letter gives and imagine yourself in the place of the recipient. Have you assumed the right manner? Have

49

you given the information required in a clear, orderly fashion? Have you made your requests clearly? As with all forms of writing, some forethought and planning are needed. (Note: A friendly letter should not contain the address of the person you are writing to and should end with 'Yours sincerely,' 'With best wishes,' or something similar—keep your 'fun' endings for your close friends and relations.)

9 Useful terms

GRAMMATICAL

Language employs the following units: **(i)** single words, **(ii)** phrases, **(iii)** clauses, **(iv)** sentences, **(v)** paragraphs.

1 Parts of speech (i.e. the different jobs done by words)

(a) A **noun** names a person, thing or quality:
e.g. boy, John, brick, beauty, decision.

(b) A **pronoun** stands in place of a noun (to avoid repeating it):
e.g. he, him, me, it, they, them, you, anyone, who, whom.

(c) A **verb** expresses an action (or state of being):
e.g. he *ran,* he *is* . . ., I *will go.*
(It has several tenses which show when the action takes place.)

(d) An **adjective** describes a noun (or pronoun). It can either stand in front of a noun or refer back to it:
e.g. a *black* cat; *my own* work; the *quick brown* fox; the street is *long.*

(e) An **adverb** usually 'modifies' a verb, telling how, where, when or why an action is done. (It can also modify an adjective or another adverb.) Except for very common adverbs, it usually ends in '-ly':
e.g. He ran *quickly*; (*very* good; *extremely* well)

(f) A **conjunction** joins, or shows the relationship between, words, phrases or clauses (see 5(b) below):
e.g. fish *and* chips; poor *but* honest; for better *or* for worse; he played well, *although* he was injured.

(g) A **preposition** introduces a phrase and is followed by a noun or pronoun (which it 'governs'):
e.g. Put it *on* the table; *by* air; *up* the pole; *over* the hills; *between* you and me

(h) An **interjection** is an exclamatory word (or phrase). It can be taken out of the sentence without destroying the sense:
e.g. *Well, er, no, oh dear, ugh*!

Nouns and pronouns as 'subject', 'direct object' and 'complement'

The **subject** is the person or thing doing the action (or being something):

e.g. *Jack* built the house. *He* hit me. *She* was a nurse.

The **direct object** is the person or thing affected by the action. (It answers the question 'Whom?' or 'What?')

e.g. Jack built *the house*. (The object—'house'—is what he built.)
He hit *me*.

The **complement** completes the sense of verbs like 'to be', 'to become', and 'to seem':

e.g. He is *an actor*.

The **personal pronouns** in the subject (nominative) case are as follows (the object—accusative—pronouns are given only where they differ):

	Singular (i.e. one)	**Plural** (i.e. more than one)
1st person	I (me)	we (us)
2nd person	you	you
3rd person	he/she/it (him/her)	they (them)

2 Phrases

A phrase is a group of words (two or more) which acts as a noun, adjective or adverb:

e.g. *To write well* requires practice. (The italicised phrase acts as a noun, 'subject' of the verb 'requires'.)
The boy *wearing the blue vest* came second. (Adjective phrase describing the noun 'boy'.)
Put it *on the table*. (Adverb phrase, telling where the action is to be done.)

3 Simple sentences

A simple sentence contains one finite verb, i.e. a verb used with its subject. The subject, in person and number, determines the form of the verb:

e.g. John *sings* well.

(A finite verb may consist of several verbs which make up its tense:

e.g. John *should have been playing,* but he was ill.)

4 Clauses

A clause is a group of words containing a finite verb. There are two basic types:

(a) Main clause—the 'backbone' of the sentence. It often makes a simple sentence on its own (but see noun clauses below).

(b) Subordinate clause—this, like a phrase, acts as an adjective, adverb or noun, and depends upon the main clause.

5 Types of subordinate clause

(a) Adjective clause

e.g. The man *who called yesterday* must have been a salesman. (The italicised words describe 'the man'.)

I found the book *(that) I had been searching for*. (Describes 'book'.)

He was absent on the day *when it happened*. (Describes 'day'.)

(b) Adverb clause

There are various kinds:

(i) Time:

e.g. The crowd cheered *when the Queen appeared.* (When?)

(ii) Place:

e.g. He hid the gold *where no one would find it.* (Where?)

(iii) Reason:

e.g. He won *because he had more stamina.* (Why?)

(iv) Purpose:

e.g. He worked hard *so that he would pass his exam.* (With what intention?)

(v) Result:

    e.g. They played so well *that they won the cup*. (With what result?)

(vi) Condition:

    e.g. You will succeed *if you try hard*. (On what condition?)

(vii) Concession:

    e.g. *Although they played well*, they still lost. (In spite of what?)

(viii) Manner:

    e.g. They did *as they pleased*. (How?)

(ix) Degree (or **comparison**):

    e.g. He sings better *than I do*. (To what extent? Compared with what?)

(c) The **noun clause** may

  (i) be the **subject** of the main verb:

    e.g. *Why he did it* remains a mystery.

  (ii) be the **direct object** of the main verb:

    e.g. I do not know *whether he will come*.

  (iii) be the **complement** of a verb of being:

    e.g. This is *how we do it*.

  (iv) be **in apposition to** a previous noun or pronoun (i.e. when enlarging upon or re-stating it):

    e.g. The idea *that he could be guilty* never crossed our minds.

    It never crossed our minds *that he was guilty*.

  (v) follow a **preposition**:

    e.g. The point of *what he said* eludes me.

    He gave an account of *when it happened*.

In all the above examples in **(a)**, **(b)** and **(c)**, the words *not* italicised form the main clause.

A sentence containing a main clause and one or more subordinate clauses is called a **complex** sentence. A sentence containing two or more main clauses (joined by 'and', 'but', 'or') is called a **compound** sentence; it may also contain subordinate clauses.

6 Paragraphs

A paragraph is a set of sentences (sometimes just one) developing *one* topic. (Make sure you indent the first line clearly, but see Section 8, sub-section 3(c) for letters.)

7 Non-finite verb-forms

These are *incomplete* forms.

(a) The **infinitive**:

e.g. *to walk, to be considered, to have seen*

(b) Participles. The present participle ends in '-ing'; the past in '-ed' (usually).

A participle may

     (i) act as an adjective:

        e.g. a talking doll

    (ii) introduce an adjective phrase:

        e.g. Talking very loudly, they got on the train.

   (iii) help form a finite verb with other verb-parts:

        e.g. I had been talking to him.

Note: the '-ing' ending may denote a gerund (a *noun*):

e.g. Talking is forbidden.

8 Active and passive

When the subject is performing the action, the verb is said to be in the 'active voice':

e.g. Jack *built* the house.

When the subject is suffering the action, the verb is said to be in the 'passive voice':

e.g. The house *was built* by Jack.

9 Transitive and intransitive verbs

A **transitive** verb takes an object:

e.g. He woke *his brother*. She boiled *an egg*. (Objects italicised.)

An **intransitive** verb does not:

e.g. He awoke. The water boiled.

10 Indirect objects

The indirect object is the person (or thing) *to* or *for* whom the action is done:

e.g. Pass the ball to *him*. He gave *me* a book. ('me' means 'to me'.)

11 Prefixes

A prefix is a small group of letters (often from Latin or Greek) put at the beginning of a word to alter its meaning:

e.g. *mis*fire; *anti*-aircraft; *extra*ordinary

12 Suffixes

A suffix is a group of letters attached to the end of a word to change its function or its meaning:

e.g. The suffix '-ly' turns an adjective into an adverb: 'careful' (adjective) becomes 'carefully' (adverb).

e.g. 'wright' (meaning 'workman') as in 'wheelwright' and 'playwright'.

LITERARY

(a) Imagery creates vivid pictures or sensations in the mind by likening one thing to another; it includes metaphors and similes. (A poem may be an extended image or set of images.)

(b) A **simile** brings out a point (or points) of likeness between two different things. It is usually introduced by the word 'like' or 'as':

e.g. Her skin was *as white as snow*.
His hand was trembling *like a leaf*.

(c) A **metaphor** is a condensed simile (without the word 'like' or 'as'). One thing is said to *be* the other thing with which it is compared.

e.g. The train *snaked* its way up the valley.
That boy is an *ass*.

(d) Personification is treating an abstract quality (like Justice or Honour) as if it were human:

e.g. Hope had grown grey hairs.

It is also commonly used to endow non-human things with human feelings:

e.g. The kettle sang merrily.

('Pathetic fallacy' is ascribing human feelings to Nature:

e.g. the angry winds, the kind old sun.)

(e) A **symbol** is an object (or set of objects) standing for some idea:

e.g. The *cross* is the symbol of Christianity.

(f) An **allegory** is a story which carries another and deeper meaning; the story stands for or suggests something else:

e.g. 'The Ancient Mariner' is an allegory about guilt.
'Animal Farm' is a political allegory.

(An allegory is a longer version of a parable.)

(g) A **pun** is a play on words, either on two meanings of the same word, or on words sounding alike:

e.g. Drilling holes is *boring*.
Was King Kong the original urban *guerrilla*?

(h) Hyperbole is exaggeration for effect:

e.g. Dinner took *ages*.

(i) A **paradox** is a saying which seems to contradict itself; its apparent nonsense, however, emphasises a truth:

e.g. More haste, less speed.

(j) A **euphemism** is a mild or indirect way of describing an unpleasant or embarrassing thing:

e.g. He passed away; a water-closet

(k) Irony

    (i) Verbal—when you mean the opposite of what the words state:

        e.g. You're a nice one!
        Antony in 'Julius Caesar' calls Caesar's assassins 'honourable men' but means the opposite.

    (ii) Dramatic—when the audience knows something that one or all of the characters on the stage don't know.

57

(l) Onomatopoeia is using words which, through their own *sound*, imitate or suggest the sound of what they describe:

e.g. miaow, buzz; the blare of trumpets; the murmuring of innumerable bees

(m) Alliteration is the repeating of sounds (usually consonants at the beginnings of words) to echo the sense or sound of the thing described:

e.g. the stuttering rifle's rapid rattle . . .

The fair breeze blew, the white foam flew,
The furrow followed free; . . .

(Assonance is repeating vowel sounds for a similar purpose.)